TACKLING LIFE

TACKLING LIFE

The true story of a footballing
bad lad made good

Charlie Oatway

SHORTLIST

First published in 2011 by
Transworld Publishers
This Large Print edition published
2011 by AudioGO Ltd
by arrangement with
Transworld Publishers

ISBN 978 1 405 62304 9

This book is a work of non-fiction
based on the experiences and
recollections of the author. The
author has stated to the publishers
that the contents of this book
are true

British Library Cataloguing in Publication Data available

Printed and bound in Great Britain by the MPG Books Group

ACKNOWLEDGEMENTS

I would like to thank the following people who have helped me in their own way to get me where I am today.

To begin with I thank Ritchie Jacobs from back home who got me into the pro game in the first place. Then the next biggest influence was Micky Adams who signed me for Brighton and Hove Albion. Then following on from Micky I want to thank all of the directors at the club, and in particular Dick Knight, Martin Perry, Derek Chapman, Ken Brown, Tony Bloom (Mr Chairman) and his brother Darren. Also a special mention to Paul Camillin, the Albion's Press Officer, who has managed to get me through a couple of scrapes! All of these people have been so supportive to me over my career.

I thank my wife and kids who have

been through all of the ups and downs together with me.

Finally I would like to thank Alan Sanders who has helped me to write this book, and we had so much fun doing it. He pushed me to focus on my literacy and numeracy skills and also helped me to achieve all of my football qualifications. He has been like a mentor to me and has led me through the difficult times.

For everyone else you are either mentioned in the book, or you'll be in the next one!

CHAPTER ONE

PENTONVILLE PRISON

To me, the summons for a court case in London on a Monday morning in 1994 was not a major problem. How could I have known at the time that it was to be the worst moment in my life? You see, I was playing professional football for Cardiff City at the time, and although I had been charged with GBH I was reliably informed (or so I thought) by my brief, that the most I would get was community service or a fine.

I had played for Cardiff on the Saturday, and after the game I told the manager, Terry Yorath, that I had to go to court in London the following Monday. I said that I would be back for training on the Tuesday. I explained that when I was living in London before I'd signed for Cardiff, I had got involved in a fight when my mate, who is Afro-Caribbean, was racially abused. We both piled in, won the fight and didn't think much more of it. Unfortunately the police did, and if I didn't go to London they would come and arrest me at the training ground.

Terry was brilliant and promised that he and the club would do all they could to keep it out of the papers. He said that he would see me on the Tuesday when I got back. I was so confident that I would be back in a few days that I told my wife, Sonya, to stay in Cardiff and not to bother travelling with me.

The train down to London was a good time for me to relax. I had only been at Cardiff for two months and in some ways I had become a local hero. I had been playing well and my face had been plastered on the side of local buses to advertise something or other.

2

Even when the judge said my full name, 'Anthony Phillip David Terry Frank Donald Stanley Gerry Gordon Steven James Oatway, you are sentenced to six months imprisonment', I still wasn't too worried. This was because he went on to say, 'It will be reduced by one month as it's your first offence, and another month for helping with the police inquiries.'

I was sure he would continue to reel off the months and let me go, or finish by saying that it was a suspended sentence. Instead, he finished by saying, 'I hereby sentence you to four months imprisonment. Take him down.' I was then handcuffed by the two policemen on either side of me and they led me downstairs to a cell and slammed the door.

My mind was racing. They told me I was in a holding cell, and that they would have to ring round the prisons to find out where I would be staying.

I had so many things going on inside my head.

For a start I was angry that my mate who I had stuck up for in the fight didn't turn up at court to tell them what had happened. Sonya, my wife, had tried to get hold of him, and when she did he said he'd got the dates mixed up and couldn't make it. My mate went on to play for QPR (Queens Park Rangers) and I suppose he didn't want anything to get in the way of his chance of becoming a professional footballer.

I also felt cheated because, not only did he not turn up, but also there were no witnesses in court and everything was just read out from statements.

I felt very hard done by as my close family friend Dennis Wise had just been let off a six-month prison sentence for GBH towards a taxi driver. If a high-profile footballer like him could be let off, why couldn't I?

4

I was now really worried about which prison they would send me to. I was hoping it would be Wormwood Scrubs as I knew a few people in there who could make sure I was all right. I was also worried about Sonya and wondered how she'd cope with it all. I knew I had really let her down and that she didn't deserve any of this.

People have asked me since whether I was worried about being beaten up or abused by other prisoners, but that was never a concern of mine. I would fight any man if I had to. I had too many other things to worry about, like what would happen to my football career? I had only just made it and now I seemed to have blown it.

After what felt like three or four hours they told me I would be going to Pentonville and not the Scrubs as I had hoped. I still have vivid memories of being put inside the police van. There were other prisoners in there, but everyone was squashed into tiny compartments where there was no room at all. You can see out into the street through a small window but no one can see you. I remember all the noise in the van on the way to Pentonville. The journey only lasted about an hour, but it felt a lot longer as the other prisoners were banging and shouting all the way there.

When we arrived I was led through the gates into the reception area, and once I'd been given my prison uniform, I was interviewed. Things didn't get any better then because when I told the officer that I was a professional footballer he didn't believe me. 'Well, that's a first,' he said. 'I've had people tell me they are the Prime Minister but never a professional footballer.'

A few hours later, the prison officer who had interviewed me told me he was also a goalkeeping coach and had worked with Terry Yorath when he was at Swansea. He had done some checking up on me and apologised for not believing that I was a footballer. He then promised he would look after me and make sure I stayed fit for when I got out. This was my first glimmer of hope. He also told me that although I had been sentenced to four months, I would be out in two if I behaved myself.

In many ways I was lucky. I was put in a cell with a Rastafarian who I got on well with and the prison officer who'd interviewed me kept his word and made sure I got the best jobs. The other prison officers were blunt but never rude to me, so there was no problem there, but I struggled with panic attacks and the feeling that I couldn't cope for the first few days.

It wasn't long before I was taken to another cell, which I would share with an armed robber. I got on well with him but the thing that helped me the most was a visit from my uncle Terry. He had been in prison many times and said he'd do anything to put himself behind bars rather than see me suffering. He also gave me a reality check, saying, 'You're only in there for a shit, shower and shave, then you'll be out.'

In fact this was the message I got from most of the prisoners I spoke to. They said that as I was only in prison for such a short time, I shouldn't worry about it. Some of them were serving up to twenty years, so I couldn't really expect any sympathy from them, not that I wanted any.

Prison was horrible. There were lots of things that made me depressed. When I was first led into prison, the sight of dead cockroaches lying on the ground outside really got to me. I couldn't cope with the fact that the only topic of conversation in prison seemed to be about the length of time people had to serve. What was I doing in this place?

The jobs I was given included being on reception helping to hand out prison clothes to newcomers, boxing up their own clothes and taking them down to the stores. A plus point of this job was that I was able to spend long periods of time outside my cell, which was a much better deal than most of the prisoners got. It also meant that while I was there I was able to meet every prisoner who arrived. As I was the one to give them their supplies, it meant that in some sense I was doing something for them, and because of that I pretty much got on with everyone. Those who didn't have jobs, which was about 80 per cent of the prisoners, had to spend long periods of time banged up inside a cell. This, in my opinion, is no good for them or anyone else.

As prisons are full of criminals, lots of bad stuff goes on in there. I never really saw much violence myself, although there were one or two nasty incidents. One man was sliced across the face with a broken dinner tray for pushing in the food queue. Even for someone like me who had been in a few fights, that shook me but also made me realise the tension and danger that comes with prison life.

The other incident was far more serious. As I was only sentenced for a short time, and because I got on with everyone, most of the inmates seemed to want to keep me out of trouble. It is commonly known that when a 'nonce' (someone who has been found guilty of committing a sex crime, usually with children) comes into a prison, the other prisoners try to beat them up any time they can. When it happened this time, some of the prisoners made sure I was sent on a wild-goose chase to get me out of the way while they gave the nonce a good hiding.

I only found out what had happened when I got back from the made-up job, which meant I was completely in the clear. I was glad they had kept me out of the way so that no one could point the finger at me. It just shows you what a dangerous place prison can be.

*   *   *

After a month my appeal came up, which could have gone any of three ways. If I lost the appeal I could have been given a longer sentence, or I might have had to start the sentence again. On the other hand, I could have been found not guilty, in which case I'd be let out straight away.

Quite simply, I was not prepared to take the risk of the first two outcomes, so I cancelled the appeal. I would rather keep my head down and just serve the remaining month. To me it was an easy choice.

When the day finally came for me

to be released, I was allowed to leave at 7 in the morning, which is unusual as prisoners are normally let out at about 11 o'clock. This was because I got on well with the prison officers and they said they would let me go first thing. Leaving prison did not make me feel brilliant. Instead, I just felt numb from the whole experience, which had really shaken me and changed my whole outlook on life.

When I was younger and often in trouble, the thought of prison didn't worry me. Many of my relatives and friends had been there at some point, and I thought it was a likely place for me to end up. Now it had happened to me, I knew that I had to avoid prison at all costs. I had tasted the good life as a professional footballer. I knew that I was never ever going back to prison.

CHAPTER TWO

'THE BUSH'

I suppose in a way, whether I liked it or not, from the minute I was born my life was always going to be different to that of most people.

It didn't help that my dad decided to have a £50 bet with a friend that he would name me after the eleven members of the Queens Park Rangers first team. Thanks, Dad! What an idiot. So why was I called Charlie? Well, when my aunt came to the hospital to visit my mum and me, she said that I looked more like 'a right little Charlie'. My mum and everyone else agreed, so that's the way it stayed. Still, as long as you won the £50 bet, Dad!

When I think about it, the local police probably thought it was my dad, Tony, who was the right little

Charlie, although they might have used something a bit stronger to describe him. He was a 'totter' (a scrap-metal merchant), who topped up his income by stealing. As a result, he's spent half his life in prison. He and his brother George were both sent to borstal at the age of twelve, where they spent two years, so not exactly a great start.

Having said that, it must have been difficult for both of them when they were growing up. Their dad (my grandfather) had spent most of his adult life either in the army or in prison. So many of my dad's and uncle's teenage years were spent trying to look after their sisters as well as my grandmother, who was ill with cancer for a couple of years.

We had a massive family network in and around Shepherd's Bush in west London. That was a rough neighbourhood in those days. Everyone I met growing up in 'the Bush', as we called it, seemed to be

14

related to us and was introduced as a 'cousin' or 'uncle'. The family was full of colourful characters and the Oatway name seemed well known. My dad Tony and Uncle George were both successful boxers in their teens. As I was growing up, my dad got me interested in all sports, which meant staying up late to watch everything on TV from darts to test cricket.

My dad wasn't too strict, but he wouldn't let us get away with much in the house (when he was there). He never hit us; shouting would do the trick because I didn't like to cross him. He tried to point me in the right direction away from the police and was keen to show me that prison should be avoided.

Dad had no favourites in our family, but he was very keen for me to visit him in prison. It wasn't just so we could stay in regular contact, but also, I think, he wanted me to see, at an early age, that prison wasn't a nice place to be. Prison was to my dad what Fletcher from the TV series *Porridge* called 'an occupational hazard'. It was just part of his life of crime.

It was quite common to see someone I knew, or was related to, in prison. I remember hearing some of my relations moaning to one another at a family gathering years later that one of my aunts wasn't 'one of us' because none of her children had been to prison!

Deep down I think my dad accepted that if anyone from our family was going to get into trouble it would probably be me. The youngest of the family with two older brothers and two older sisters, I was more mouthy than the others. I would often get caught fighting at school or getting into trouble some other way.

Thinking back, I have a lot of sympathy for my mum, Doreen. She worked hard as the manageress of a local Curtis shoe shop, as well as trying to keep the family together when my dad was in prison. She was from a tough working-class background in west London and was used to hard work, but I doubt she'd been expecting this kind of lifestyle.

When I was about eight or nine, I was taken to football matches by my dad and one of my older brothers, Roy. My home was in Loftus Road, the first house next to the Queens Park Rangers (QPR) football stadium. I would often climb over the fence to watch the match with my brothers and cousins. Our dog stood guard and tried to ward off anyone trying to do the same. We were worried that if too many people got in for free they'd get caught and we would be stopped.

Throughout the hard times, family loyalty kept us together. I remember my dad giving money to family, friends or neighbours who had just come out of prison to help them get back on their feet. Everyone pulled together and my family got the same help when my dad was in prison.

We lived in a big council house and we always had cousins staying with us, normally because one parent was in prison. We got on well with our visitors and there were never any problems between us. We were raided by the police a few times, too, but I don't remember them ever finding any of the stolen goods they were looking for.

My brother Roy, who is eight years older than me, has always been really supportive throughout my life, particularly when I was younger. He worked really hard at school and got good qualifications. When he left home he moved out of 'the Bush' and went into banking, where he's had a good career ever since.

Despite the differences in our lives and characters, Roy has remained close to me. He regularly drove miles after work to give me reading and writing lessons, as well as driving me to football training and matches.

My other brother Barry, who is ten years older than me and a qualified gas fitter, was just as supportive. He always looked after me when it came to money and clothes. He also got in the odd fight for me when I got into trouble.

I remember once when I was about ten, I was with my family in the Old Oak Club in East Acton and I was up to my usual trick of annoying people. This time it was a girl. When her brother came over to tell me off, Barry stepped in to help me. I could see that Barry was getting more and more upset as the two got into a heated argument. I tried to stand in between them, but wasn't able to stop them trading punches.

I was in the middle, about twelve inches smaller than the two of them, trying to hold Barry back. It's an image I'll never forget and one of my earliest memories of feeling guilty. Whoops! Perhaps I shouldn't have started that.

Living in 'the Bush' in terraced houses that led straight out onto the pavement helped us get to know our neighbours. In some cases this was good because it helped create a close-knit community. Many of the local parents would sit on their doorsteps and chat to their neighbours while their kids played football in the streets. Some people didn't think this was such a great idea, though, because their cars would get hit by the footballs and they'd come out on the street ranting and raving.

For me, between the ages of seven and twelve, having people sitting out on the streets was a great chance to earn some money. I became quite good at break-dancing and family and friends would pay £1 each to watch me perform. My friend Andy Colbert and I used to go to clubs like the Old Oak in Acton and earn money by break-dancing on the dance floor. That was a nice little earner.

Whatever I did, there was always trouble round the corner. I regularly got into fights, and because I was small, I lost as many as I won. I remember one fight when I was eleven against a boy who scratched me quite badly all over my face. When I got home I was surprised to find that my family were more worried about whether or not I'd won than how I was. A lot of the time I was told I had to join in fights even though I wasn't that keen.

As I got a bit older, I progressed from being a bad fighter to an even worse crook. My first failure was at thirteen when two friends and I decided to mug the 'tally man'. The 'tally man' used to come around to people's houses to trade, buying and selling clothes, offering loans and so on. We knew that he always carried money, most of which would have been taken from our neighbours to

21

repay their loans. We planned to steal this cash and give it back to them, like young Robin Hoods.

My friends Richard and Spencer and I waited for three hours for the 'tally man' to come by, but he never showed up. We were freezing cold and in the end we gave up. Sadly for us, he had been delayed, and ten minutes after we got home there was a knock on the door. There we were in our black clothes, still trying to take off the shoe polish we'd put on our faces as a disguise. I'm sure that having seen us in this state he knew what we'd been planning, but, instead of robbing him, our families ended up paying over the money we owed him.

It was around this time that Richard thought of another great chance for earning some money. It involved going to a parade of shops near Victoria Station in central London. The plan was that we'd do the simple task of smashing the shop windows and grabbing some expensive cameras. Unfortunately, we weren't strong enough to break the glass as we didn't realise it was reinforced. Before we knew it the police had turned up. There was a helicopter overhead and we got caught. Richard went straight on remand, as he was older than me, but I was let off with a caution.

My dad was disappointed with me on two counts. First, for getting involved in crime despite his warnings, and second (and perhaps more importantly, for him) for failing. He must have felt I was dragging the family name through the gutter by being such a bad criminal, and after everything he'd done to build his reputation. To be fair, I didn't want to get involved in crime: I was just easily led. Older boys only took me along because I was under age and could take the blame. Well, that's my story anyway.

Now and then my troubles spilt

over into family life. When I was fourteen and my brother Barry was out, I 'borrowed' his car. I stopped at a zebra crossing to let a woman walk across the road, and I couldn't believe my bad luck when she looked through the windscreen to see who was driving. It wouldn't have mattered but it was my Aunt Rita!

I drove a few miles away and ditched the car, but by this time Aunt Rita had told Barry, who was on the warpath and out looking for me. Before long, everyone in the local area seemed to have heard about the incident. Barry eventually caught up with me and gave me a real hiding. It was probably because my aunt had told him I was a better driver than him because I stopped for people at zebra crossings!

CHAPTER THREE

ACTING THE FOOL AT SCHOOL

When I look back at my early years growing up, life was quite hectic. I was the youngest of a family with five kids and there were always people coming to visit. Some of them were welcome whilst others, like the police, weren't.

Like any kid going to school for the first time, I was a bit nervous, but I soon got into the swing of things. I went to Miles Coverdale School in Shepherd's Bush and I have very happy memories of when I first started. I got on well with the teachers and the other kids, and I was learning new things all the time.

Between the ages of five and eight, I enjoyed school and had no idea that I had a problem with reading and writing which would affect my whole life. At the time, I didn't think I was different to anyone else. Most of the writing I remember doing was copying off the board, and for some strange reason I quite enjoyed that. It wasn't until I was about nine that I began to realise a lot of the other children in my class were getting ahead of me with their lessons. I noticed it most when we were asked to write our own stories. I could make them up all right in my head, but I couldn't get them down on paper. My spelling was all over the place and it took me so long to write anything that I pretty much lost interest.

While I may not have been doing well in the classroom I was achieving something outside of it. I was playing a lot of football with other boys who lived on my estate and I found I had a bit of a talent for it. I suppose playing with lads who were older than me helped. I was smaller than them, but I soon learned how to make sure this didn't stop me from being one of the best. People have asked me since whether I liked playing other sports, but I was only interested in football, football, football.

There was a guy called Les who worked for QPR and he used to come and do an after-school club with us. There was no school football team, but I knew by the time I was eight that I was as good as any of the eleven-year-olds I was playing with. The school sent me for trials for the West London District team and I got in. I also played for Harrow Boys Club and the Bedfont Eagles.

The manager of the Eagles used to come all the way over from Bedfont, pick me up for the games and then drive me home again afterwards. The round-trip must have been at least twenty miles. Knowing that someone was prepared to do that for me, even though I was still at primary school, certainly made me feel good about myself.

When I look back, the football was a great education for me in itself. All the kids I played with, and those from my school, came from different racial backgrounds. Not that it mattered to any of us as we all learned to get along just by playing football together. The colour of people's skin was never an issue.

But with my dad constantly in and out of prison, life was hard for my mum. She not only had to raise us but also hold down a full-time job at the shoe shop. I'm not sure if people coming in and out of our house daily, to visit or to stay, made her life any more difficult, but she managed to look after us well.

Although my football was going from strength to strength, everything inside the classroom seemed to be going wrong for me. As my frustration with reading and writing grew, so my behaviour got worse. The teachers started to take me out of the classroom when I misbehaved and I soon decided that this was the best option. When I was sent outside into the corridor to work, I couldn't be made to look stupid in front of the other kids. For me the corridor was a comfort zone, and if it meant misbehaving to get there, so be it.

Of course all of this came at a cost. I wasn't learning anything, but that wasn't the thing that worried me at the time. What really got to me was that because I played up, I was never allowed to go on school trips. I remember crying and pleading with the teachers to let me go, but the answer was always no.

I have to admit that it wouldn't be right to put all of my misbehaviour down to my struggles with reading and writing. I enjoyed being a tearaway. Quite a few members of my family, and the people I hung around with, were tearaways too. I suppose it just goes to show that you're either born into that role or you fall into it.

On one occasion a friend and I broke into a log cabin on the school playing field where all the PE equipment was kept. We didn't want to steal anything, we just thought it would be fun to break in. The head teacher went mad and made us stand up in assembly while he told everybody what we'd done. I was so embarrassed I cried. The school also told my mum, and I got a right telling off as soon as I got home as well.

By the time I finished at primary school, I had a reputation not only for being badly behaved but for struggling with the work. To be honest, I think the staff at Miles Coverdale were glad to get rid of me, and I suppose I can't blame them.

Like most of the kids from my primary school I went on to Burlington Danes secondary school in Wood Lane, Shepherd's Bush, which just happens to be next to

Wormwood Scrubs Prison. At least visiting any of my relations when they got put away in there didn't involve a long journey!

A few weeks before I left Miles Coverdale, a couple of teachers from Burlington Danes came to visit us at home. They said they'd read all the reports about me and seen samples of my work. They didn't think there would be a problem when I started at secondary school. The teachers said that although I might be a bit behind most of the other kids, it wouldn't take me long to catch up. My mum was delighted and so was I. It gave me the lift I needed and I felt I had the chance of a new start and that this time I wasn't going to blow it.

Sadly, though, it wasn't to be. I was nervous, but there was also the added pressure that I would get found out again. I was worried that the teachers would discover I was terrible at reading and writing.

It didn't take long for me to realise

31

that I just couldn't do the work. First I decided that the easiest way out was to copy someone else, but that didn't solve anything, so I just went back to the only solution I knew: I started messing about. I got into a lot of trouble with the teachers for general misbehaviour, but I didn't get into fights with the other kids.

My form teacher wasn't much help either. She was an Australian who was only in England for a year and she spent most of the time telling us she couldn't wait to get back home.

The final straw came when I fell out with one of my teachers over reading. I completely lost it, picked up a chair and threw it at him. From then on there was no way back. I got booted out of school having only lasted one term of the second year.

The education authorities decided that I should go to Wood Lane Special School, but I knew from the minute I walked into the place that I didn't belong there. All the other kids had either physical disabilities (quite a few were in wheelchairs or had cerebral palsy) or had mental health issues. Even though I was young, I knew that the problems they had, which I felt really sorry about, were not the same as my problems with learning. The staff offered to pick me up in the blue school bus, but I said I'd rather walk. The truth was I didn't want to be seen in a school bus for children with problems.

The school itself was right next to Burlington Danes, so while I was there I took care not to be seen by any of the kids from my old school, and when it was break time I avoided going into the playground.

My behaviour at this second new school was really good, but because I wasn't actually ill they told me I had to leave and go to a place called a 'Projects Special Unit'. This is a place for children with serious behaviour problems and there was no way my mum would let me go there.

Mum said that this school was a breeding ground for criminals, and I think to a certain extent she was right. She fought the local authority tooth and nail to stop me from being sent there, but they refused to give in. For my mum there was only one solution: I would have to stay at home. So from the age of thirteen I didn't go to school again.

My brother Roy came down on a weekly basis to help me with my reading and writing as my mum couldn't afford a tutor, but I never took any exams. If I'm honest, life away from school was a bit boring. I had one friend who used to wait until his parents had gone to work, then bunk off school and come round to my place, but we didn't really get up to much. I spent my time watching daytime television and waiting for the other kids to get out of school. Then we'd go on to the Suttons

Estate in Notting Hill to play and hang around.

When I look back I know I let myself down, but I can't help thinking that the authorities let me down, too. I don't think this sort of thing would happen nowadays, but I may be wrong.

CHAPTER FOUR

BAD LAD ON THE STREETS

People have often asked me what I got up to when I was hanging around. Well, for one thing I never smoked or took drugs. None of that appealed to me, and to be honest it wasn't something many of my mates got into either. I did drink a bit, but not much more than most fourteen- or fifteen-year-olds. We just wanted to have a laugh, and we messed about, mostly at each other's expense. I have to admit there were a few activities we shouldn't have been involved in, though, like breaking and entering and fighting.

At fourteen, I was very grateful when my brother-in-law's dad offered me a job selling fish tanks at a shop in east London. A lot of kids who were thrown out of school worked there from time to time and we all earned £50 a week. I used to give the money to my mum so that she could keep it and give it back to me when I needed it.

When I was fifteen, I got a job with my cousin Warren in a warehouse in Notting Hill doing painting and decorating, but by this time my football was beginning to take off in quite a big way. A school in Holland Park called Cardinal Vaughan allowed me to play for them, even though I'd never even been to the school. Slightly corrupt I know, but I wasn't complaining. If anyone ever asked me why I didn't go to school, I used to say I was a bad kid and no school would have me, which I suppose was basically true.

*   *   *

Two of the people who helped me most with my football career in the early days were my cousin Terry Oatway and a player called Wally Downes. They were the best of mates and used to hang around together. Wally played semi-professionally for Wimbledon and was also on the coaching staff there, so he and Terry arranged for me to have a trial. After that, the club agreed to let me train there for a month. My football impressed them so they got me to sign some schoolboy forms, which for someone who wasn't attending school seemed a bit strange!

Life at Wimbledon went well, although one of the coaches seemed to have a problem with me. It all started while we were on a pre-season trip to Sweden. One time I arrived back from a night out two hours after curfew. Although there were a few of us, he picked on me rather than anyone else, claiming I was the ringleader.

When we got back to England, he

took it upon himself to look into my background, and the more digging he did, the worse it got for me. He found out that there had been an incident with a taxi driver when a few of us did a runner after getting a cab back to the estate. We'd paid some of the bill but didn't have enough money to pay the full amount. The cab driver went ballistic and said he'd come back with some other drivers to sort it out, which he did. There was a bit of a fight and the police were called.

For some reason they picked on me and shoved me in a van, then they drove me to the police station. They were a bit over the top when they took me out of the van and bundled me into the cell, and one of them kicked me in the head. Then they put white forensic overalls on me. When my brief arrived, I told him what had happened, and although the police denied it, my brief noticed some blood on my overalls, which could only have come from my head. The police decided to drop all charges because they knew they could get into serious trouble, and in the end I was cleared.

But that didn't stop the coach from finding out about it, and he started asking me all sorts of questions. There was nothing that bad to find out, though my friends and I were involved in 'borrowing' a few cars from local garage showrooms (I'll never understand why they always left the keys in the cars!). For the record, we never damaged any of them and just used to leave them in a nearby road.

Although a couple of my friends got in trouble with the police over that, I was never caught, so the coach could only go on hearsay. That, however, didn't stop him making sure I was seen as the 'bad boy' of the youth team. The year I joined the team, 1988, was when Wimbledon were at their peak, with a reputation for having a few 'lively' players, like Vinnie Jones, Dennis Wise and John Fashanu, so in a way I fitted in quite well.

At the end of the 1989/90 season, when I was sixteen, the club decided to let me go rather than sign me as a trainee. It was a blow because I'd really thought I had a chance of going on to the next stage. Instead, I signed for a non-league club, Yeading, at semi-pro level and had a really good pre-season.

A scout for Derby County saw me play and asked me up there for a week's trial. Things went well and at the end of the week they said they'd be back in touch. The trouble was they kept dithering and wouldn't make up their minds. Yeading spoke to them and said they ought to let me know one way or another, but I told Yeading to tell them to forget it and I decided to stay with them instead.

Football aside, I was getting involved in some petty crime, mainly a bit of stealing here and there. I also had a job labouring and gardening, which mainly consisted of helping to build brick walls at the fronts and backs of people's gardens. What with that and my earnings from Yeading I was bringing in enough to get by.

Meanwhile my personal life had got a bit complicated. I'd been going out with a girl called Debbie since I was about thirteen, and when I was seventeen we had a son we called 'Charlie boy'. Debbie was from an Irish Catholic background, so an abortion was out of the question. We were lucky, though, because once she had Charlie boy, we jumped the council waiting list and got a flat in Loftus Road.

Things were going OK, but we were both too young to settle down and looking back it was never going to work. I'm no angel, but did she have a temper! I thought at times she must be a bit mad, though I guess she must have been to hook up with me in the first place.

It was when we had one of our major bust-ups that I met my wife, Sonya. I'd been separated from Debbie for a couple of months but thought we would probably get back together. Then a friend of mine arranged a blind date with his girlfriend's mate. The four of us went to a do at Yeading Football Club, funnily enough, and Sonya and I hit it off straight away. We didn't see each other for a week as the next day I was off on a pre-season tour, but when I got back we started going out. Within three months Sonya became pregnant with Talia, so by the age of nineteen I had two children with two different mothers.

It was then that I started to think I should be a bit more responsible. Sonya was eighteen and had a pretty good job with a decent wage and a company car working for British Airways in the finance department. Considering where I'd come from,

I'd done pretty well to be with someone who had such a good job.

The 1993/94 season with Yeading went really well and the football team got promoted. There were quite a few clubs looking at me, but they always seemed to come to the same conclusion: that I was too small to play in central midfield at a professional level.

At the end of that season a guy called Ritchie Jacobs, who was a community worker on the estate, somehow got me and a couple of my mates, Joe Omigie and Alan Mills, a trial at Cardiff City. I was the only one of the three of us who was invited back after the week's trial, although Joe went on to play for Brentford.

I have to say at this point what a good bloke Ritchie was to set this up for us. He could see that we were three young lads with some talent, who were pretty much wasting our lives and needed a break, and he set up the trial out of the goodness of his heart.

During the week's trial, I realised that the professionals we were training with were really no better than me. That started to build my hopes up, although in the back of my mind I was still preparing for another failure. When Cardiff asked me back for another month, I knew it was the chance I'd been waiting for, and I was going to grab it with both hands.

CHAPTER FIVE

MAKING IT, AND NEARLY BREAKING IT

When I arrived at Cardiff City Football Club in the summer of 1994, life was good. I had been given a one-year contract, which was an incredible feeling. I was confident that I had the ability, as long as I could remain free of injuries and stay out of trouble.

I knew from experience how my life might turn out if I didn't make this work, and I was determined to stay in professional football. What I didn't know was that for the next few years my life was going to be all about survival and overcoming some major hurdles.

I was on £200 a week and I really had no expenses. I was given digs on Barry Island in the Majestic Holiday

Camp. This was owned by the club chairman, Rick Wright, who'd taken it over from Butlin's in the 1980s. It was a bit strange being in the same complex as holidaymakers, but I didn't mind. I was only in there for two weeks before I was moved to a pub so I could be nearer the training ground. Finally I settled into a bed and breakfast that was owned by the manager's step-daughter and her husband. This was good because they could keep an eye on me and I couldn't get away with anything, even if I wanted to.

I settled in well at Cardiff and loved it there. I got on with the other players, most of whom were Welsh, but there were a few English players as well as a couple from Ireland. Every Friday we'd have small games with the Welsh playing the English. The tackles used to fly in, and to be quite honest some of them were horrendous. We got quite a bit of rain that summer and autumn, so the tackles were made even worse due to the slippery surface.

Of course there was lots of banter that went along with this and the manager, Eddie May, allowed it all to happen. I remember thinking that although I loved it, it didn't really seem like the right thing to be doing. There were quite a few occasions when players couldn't play on the Saturday because they'd been injured in a Friday game.

I couldn't believe my luck. I was playing in the first team and everyone at the club treated me really well. It seemed that wherever I went in Cardiff, people knew me. I was offered massive discounts whenever I went shopping and I generally got the best of everything. I wasn't just recognised in Cardiff either. I remember going into the Welsh valleys for a drink one evening and being spotted by some Swansea supporters. I didn't hang around for long. Anyone who knows about the rivalry between Cardiff and Swansea will tell you there is serious hatred between them.

With everything going so well, the last thing I wanted was my past catching up with me, so as you can imagine, the two months I spent in Pentonville Prison were a bombshell I can't put into words.

That spell inside was a true test of character for me, but it wasn't just being in prison that I was worried about, I was also concerned about the reaction of my team-mates when I got out. I shouldn't have worried, though, because on my first day back it was as if I'd never been away. They asked me what it was like inside prison and then we got straight on with the football. It was almost as if they were asking me what I'd done over the weekend.

As for worrying about the reception I would get from the Cardiff fans, I needn't have bothered about that either. I wasn't fit enough to play in the first game after my release, so instead I was taken out to the centre of the pitch before the game where I was given a standing ovation. I think the fact that my offence was GBH meant it was almost seen as part of football culture. Not that I feel proud of what I did, but I do think that sticking up for a friend while he is being racially abused isn't the worst crime in the world.

Some big changes had taken place at the club while I was in prison. By the time I was released there had been a change in both the owners and the management at Cardiff. Eddie May had been sacked and the new owners, the Kumar brothers, instructed the new manager, Kenny Hibbitt, to put me out on loan to another club.

I was sent to Coleraine in Northern Ireland. I actually preferred this to playing in the reserves at Cardiff, although the standard was way below what I was used to. All the players were part-time and the pitches weren't the best either. I was getting my full-time wages, but to be honest I wasn't that comfortable there.

Being English didn't help. Had it not been for Paul Millar, who was a fellow ex-professional at Cardiff now playing for nearby club Linfield, I would really have struggled. Our wives got on very well, so when Sonya moved out to join me it was just about bearable. I have to say that living in Northern Ireland was quite a steep learning curve. There seemed to be no police around, just the army, and there were loads of sealed-off areas, none of which was my cup of tea.

When I returned to Cardiff, I played in the reserves until the end of the season, when we were relegated to Division 4. Fortunately though, the club decided to give me another one-year contract. I've heard a lot of people in professional football say that one of the hardest things is to get an extension after your first year, so at least I'd managed to do that. The problem was I still wasn't in the first team.

One day I was playing in the reserves in an away match against Torquay, whose first-team manager happened to be my ex-boss at Cardiff, Eddie May. He asked me if I would consider a transfer, which was music to my ears. I moved down to Torquay before Christmas and went straight into the first team, and although I only played for half the season, I still managed to be awarded 'player of the year'.

That was the good news, but the bad news was that we finished bottom of the league. Fortunately for us, the champions of the Conference (the league below the main Football League), Stevenage Borough Football Club, were unable to make the ground improvements necessary for promotion, so we were saved.

* * *

At the end of the season, Eddie moved to manage Brentford and Torquay brought in Kevin Hodges. The change in management didn't have a big effect on our results, though, because they couldn't attract players to Torquay. It was a long way from anywhere and there was little chance of scouts coming to see us play, although I suppose there were always the away games. Playing away meant travelling hundreds of miles and we didn't have the money for many overnight stays.

You may think that being a professional footballer is glamorous, but it didn't feel like it then, not that I was moaning. I remember travelling by coach on a Sunday to play Hartlepool on the Tuesday. By the time we got back in the early hours of the Wednesday morning my little boy Charlie was going to school. I felt as if I had jet lag and I hadn't even left England.

One thing I was beginning to realise was that I really loved the battle of the game. In some ways it didn't matter to me that we had to scrap for every point as I was in my element. I think that's why I won player of the year the previous season: I just ran, tackled and battled for the whole ninety minutes. A nil-nil away from home was cause for celebration in my book.

I think my past may have helped me with this never-say-die attitude. I felt that playing professional football was such a fantastic thing to be doing and running around a football pitch was no hardship at all. I see a lot of lads playing today who have more talent than I ever had, but they don't have a chance in hell of making it because they don't want it enough. They lose concentration too easily and don't have that will to win.

I only lasted a few months into the 1997/98 season at Torquay before Brentford put in an offer for me. The wrangling between the clubs went on for what seemed like ages before the deal was done. When it was finally sorted I was really pleased to make the move, not least because the club was in London. Eddie May was the manager and they were playing in the division above Torquay, having just missed out on promotion to the Championship.

I have to give a quick mention to Eddie May at this point as I owe him such a lot. Over a period of three years he took me from Cardiff to Torquay and then on to Brentford. If it hadn't been for him, my professional career might have been a lot shorter. Eddie always believed in me, and as so often happens in football, when a manager moves clubs he buys players who have played under him before.

Eddie used to make me laugh. He

managed like he had played: he used to be a big centre half and he took no prisoners. He would get so mad when he was manager. His mind worked quicker than his mouth, so when he tried to say something he couldn't speak quickly enough. He couldn't even swear properly!

When I arrived at Brentford, life wasn't all a bed of roses. Dave Webb was the chairman and I was the only player he'd allowed Eddie to bring in. When the results didn't go our way, Eddie was sacked, only to be replaced by Micky Adams. The first thing Micky said to me was, 'You're not going to cause me any trouble, are you?' Talk about your reputation getting ahead of you!

I replied, 'No, why would I want to do that?' And I didn't, I just kept battling away and always trying my best. That didn't stop us getting relegated though, which meant that, had it not been for Stevenage's problems, I would have been relegated three times in three years with three different clubs. That must be some kind of record!

After that life got a little bizarre. Ron Noades took over from Dave Webb as chairman and appointed himself manager too. Ron got Ray Lewington and Terry Bullivant to help him and I have to say they did a great job. We ended up winning the league, and as I was pretty much a regular player I was offered another one-year contract. At least I'd stopped the rot on the relegation front and proved I wasn't just a player who was good in a dog fight.

In the summer of 1999, I got a call from Micky Adams, who had just become manager of Brighton Football Club. He was keen to sign me, but only as part of a package deal with Paul Watson (Watto), who played at right back with me at Brentford.

I went away on holiday that summer thinking it was a done deal, but then I got a call from Micky saying the deal could be off as Watto couldn't make up his mind. I got on the phone to Watto and told him he had to do it. In the end he agreed to sign with me and Brighton bought us both for £30,000. To this day I claim that I was bought for £20,000 and Watto for £10,000, though of course he disputes it!

Five years had passed since I'd been sent to prison. I'd known some hard times, but it seemed that finally my life was getting sorted. If you're not an avid football fan you may not have heard of the clubs I've played for, but for me it was living my childhood dream. I was a professional footballer and nothing could have been better.

CHAPTER SIX

FAMILY STRIFE

As you've probably gathered by now, quite a few members of my family and friends have lived life on the edge as far as the law is concerned. Some have spent years in and out of prison for crimes they've committed. Others have done time for crimes they weren't guilty of, though they may have been closely involved with them. Then there are others who went on trial but there wasn't enough evidence to send them down.

I'm not about to say who I think was guilty and who was innocent, because in some cases I honestly don't know. What I do know is that some of the situations my family and friends have had to live through are, to say the least, not the normal way of life.

59

I mentioned in chapter two that my dad and his brother George both had lifetimes of trouble. I was aware from an early age of my dad spending a lot of his time in jail as my mum and I were always visiting him and other members of my family in prison.

One of my earliest visits was when he was in an open prison, which he regarded as a breeze compared with some of the other prisons he'd been in. On this occasion he noticed I was particularly upset, so to cheer me up he winked at me and said it was a sort of holiday camp he was staying in to give him a break from Mum. For some reason that made me feel a lot better. He always knew how to make me laugh.

Apparently in 1966, before I was born, the police arrived when Dad was halfway through a robbery. He knew his way around the Shepherd's Bush area, so jumped across the rooftops to get away from them.

When I was told about this when I was older I was amazed: I couldn't believe a man who was too scared to drive a car could be brave enough to climb walls and jump across rooftops.

When he was escaping, he fell and broke his back. He was told he'd never walk again, but he was up and back at 'work' again six months later, after serving a short period of probation.

Another time, my dad had to go into hiding. He was on the run for a robbery and he turned to the infamous Kray twins for help. Dad had just come out of prison and during his stretch he'd made friends with Pauly Hearn, who was the Krays' cousin. My dad had pretty much looked after Pauly when they were inside, so Pauly said that if he ever needed help once he was released, he should call him. I don't think Pauly expected my dad to get in touch quite so soon, but after only a few months he was on the phone.

The Krays were based on the other side of town in the East End, which worked quite well. They put my dad, mum and brothers Roy and Barry in a flat above a tailor's, where they stayed for over two years. My dad then went back to the West End to see if it was safe, but as he was still uncertain they moved to Hastings, on the South Coast, and stayed with relations for a few more months. Finally my family returned home to west London, and by that time the police seemed to have forgotten all about it!

My dad has a sister called Sheila and she was always dripping in gold jewellery. Her husband, nicknamed 'Gollar', and my Uncle George often went out thieving together. The pair of them brought back what our family called 'parcels' for Aunt Sheila to deal with. This would mean either keeping the loot for themselves or selling the items on. At least that's what I'm told, although as I said, I couldn't swear by it!

In many ways this pattern of behaviour continued into the next generation, with me on my dad's side and my five cousins on Uncle George's side. All five of them, Terry, George, Stephen, Tony and John, have been in and out of prison throughout their lives. The crimes they've been accused of, and in some cases convicted of, range from theft to attempted murder. Each of them has served sentences of between three and seven years.

My cousin who was accused of attempted murder was John. He was accused of walking into a pub called The Pig and Whistle in Notting Hill and shooting someone at almost point blank range for grassing him up over an armed robbery. The man who was shot survived. John never went on trial as the police and the prosecutors were unable to find enough witnesses to build their case.

My dad had another sister who wanted no part of this lifestyle, and once she was grown up she left London and never came back. Even to this day I think everyone's lost touch with her.

Perhaps the worst crime committed by a member of my family in recent years was by my nephew Lee. He was convicted of murder and two attempted murders in 2006. As far as I know there had been a problem over drugs and girls and he and three other blokes went round to some guy's house to sort it out. Lee and his mates were owed money and after repeated warnings they wanted it from the trio in question there and then.

When it became clear that they weren't going to pay up, things turned nasty. There was a fight and all three of the debtors were stabbed; one ended up dead and the other two survived. Lee got two life sentences and is currently banged up in Wakefield Prison, even though he personally didn't have a knife with him at the time. He still claims he's innocent.

It may seem a bit out of order, but I found it quite funny when Lee told me they wouldn't have been caught if they hadn't been grassed up. He wasn't prepared to admit that the pink convertible they were driving at the time of the murder stood out like a sore thumb to the witnesses who gave evidence. I mean, talk about bringing attention to yourself!

I go and visit my nephew Lee in prison whenever I can as I've always been pretty close to him. In fact, it was me and his dad who talked him into giving himself up to the police.

After the crime was committed, Lee went on the run and I got a few messages from him. I thought he had no option but to turn himself in and I'm glad he did, although it was painful to know that I probably wouldn't see him except in prison for a very long time. In the end it was ruled that he should serve twenty-five years in jail.

*　　　*　　　*

When I was young, I used to spend time at the house of Jimmy and Mary Wise (Jimmy is the uncle of footballer Dennis Wise). I used to play with their son Boysie and we became really good friends. Jimmy used to be my dad's driver when he 'went to work'. I used to see Dennis quite a bit and the whole family became good friends of ours.

I remember Jimmy and Mary having really noisy neighbours at one time and, despite repeated requests, they wouldn't be quieter. In the end there was a row and the police turned up. Jimmy said Boysie and I should fight their two kids to settle it, but for some strange reason the police didn't think that was the best solution! The problem didn't go away and in the end Jimmy went round to sort it out himself. He knocked the other man out cold by hitting him with a slab of meat and was sentenced to five years in prison as a result.

Beyond my family I've had a couple of close friends who've been charged with murder. One, Ant, was found guilty and the other, Paul, walked away from court a free man. When he was in his late twenties, Ant had to serve fifteen years for a double murder that took place after another disagreement over money and drugs. Paul, on the other hand, was found not guilty of shooting a man in a nightclub. He has, however, served quite a bit of time for armed robbery.

This may sound bad, but if I had to pick the two people I've been closest to outside of my family, it would be these two mates. They've always been brilliant to me and I have tried to repay them whenever I can. They have spent a lot of their lives on the wrong side of the law, but that's just life with my friends and family.

Don't get me wrong, though. People who don't know me might think I agree with the crimes my family and friends have committed, but the truth is that I don't. I'm not trying to preach to anyone or to take the moral high-ground. I'm hardly in a position to do that but, in my view, crime just doesn't pay and I have been pretty shocked and upset by some of the things I've described.

My family has had one or two success stories, though, and I have to say that my brothers Roy and Barry are probably the best examples. They have gone on to have successful careers, despite our slightly dodgy upbringing. Meanwhile, Roy's son is so bright he'll definitely be going to university.

Whatever my family have done, we're a very close-knit unit. I'm lucky enough to have some very close friends, too, and I'll always stick by them through thick and thin. That's the way I like both to live, and play my football.

CHAPTER SEVEN

BRIGHTON ROCKS

So with prison well behind me, I arrived at Brighton and Hove Albion in the summer of 1999 feeling on top of the world. There were high expectations at the club, not only from me as a player, but from the fans as well. We all felt that Micky Adams, as the manager, was bound to be successful. The club had just moved back to a ground in the city after two years spent ground-sharing with Gillingham and everyone thought the club was about to take off.

The first game at our new place, Withdean Stadium, was certainly one to remember. We won 6–0 against Mansfield, with local boy Darren Freeman scoring a hat-trick. Sadly the rest of the season didn't turn out as planned, and we only finished twelfth. It was a bit of an anti-climax, but we had a good run at the end of the season, by which time Micky had brought in some new players. All in all I felt we'd under-achieved. We were one of the only clubs paying out good money, both in terms of transfers and players' wages, so there was really no excuse. By pre-season in the summer of 2000, I think all the players knew we could be on to something good.

Meanwhile Micky was keen to show that he was no pushover. One of his signings was a player called (funnily enough) David Cameron, who he brought in from the Army. David hadn't really delivered for us, so Micky gave him one last chance. The writing was on the wall when he started the game up at Hull and was taken off after only fifteen minutes. From then on, David spent all his time training on his own, running and running to and fro.

Micky was also pretty tough with some of the other players. I remember him taking Paul Brooker and Nathan Jones off the pitch just fifteen minutes into a game against Southend. In another match, he took our goalkeeper, Michel Kuipers, off at half-time. Having said that, Micky soon got him back involved again and Michel went on to be one of Brighton's all-time great goalkeepers.

The thing I like about Micky as a manager is that he's a man's man. He's as straight as a die and you always know where you stand. I've had plenty of arguments with him over the years, especially when he dropped me from the first team, but we still chat regularly on the phone to this day. I regard him as a top bloke as well as a top manager.

Micky liked taking us on a pre-season tour to Ireland to liven us up with a bit of the hard life. We went to a place called Ballygar and it was very dull: very few pubs, a couple of shops and nowhere to go, which is just how he wanted it. In the hotel we were staying in there were only six rooms, so some of us, including me as I was one of the youngest players, had to stay with local families. All we did for training was run up and down, and I've never met a player who likes doing that. So when we eventually played a friendly against a team called Longford we were all knackered.

The match turned out to be a nightmare and is known among those of us who were there as 'The Battle of Longford'. We weren't playing well because of all the training we'd been doing and everyone was a yard off the pace. There were arguments going on between our players. Worse still, Longford Football Club had some nugget playing up front who liked to dive in with late tackles and kept trying to kick all of us.

Micky shouted for someone to sort it out, so one of my team—Steve

Melton—took it upon himself to take the Longford player down with a two-footed tackle at chest height. All of a sudden there were twenty-two players, the subs and the managers involved in a mass brawl. I'd never seen anything like it and probably never will. One of their players grabbed me in a headlock, so I bit him. It was the only way I could get free.

The game was of course called off and we all went back to the changing rooms. As we were leaving, our assistant manager Bob Booker popped his head into the changing room of our opponents and thanked them for their warm hospitality. We could hear all these boots being flung at the door as he quickly shut it and ran on to the team bus.

We had a better time as a team abroad at the end of that 2000/01 season when we got promoted. Tony Bloom, who is now chairman of the club, said that if we won the league he would pay for us all to go to Marbella in Spain to celebrate.

It wasn't that we needed an incentive, but it stopped us from settling for second place! My biggest memory of that trip abroad is seeing Tony leaving the hotel one day and turning to all of us to say goodbye, then walking straight into a glass door that he thought was open. He didn't half hit it with a bang, poor bloke!

*   *   *

In the lead-up to the end of the season we had a massive match at home against Chesterfield. In the away match with them a few months earlier I had been sent off for a foul, even though I never made contact. We were 1–0 up at that point and eventually drew 1–1, which I blamed myself for. At the end of the game the Chesterfield players banged on our changing-room door and shouted that they would win the league. That was all the incentive we needed for the home game, as Micky kept reminding us.

To add fuel to the fire, Chesterfield were being investigated for 'bungs' (dodgy finances) by the Football League. Our fans kept waving money at them and there was a lot of tension in the atmosphere at the match. We won after a headed goal by our captain, Danny Cullip, and at the end of the game we gave them some stick as we walked off. This was just to pay the other team back for the game at their place.

By the time we got to the Portakabin changing rooms fighting had broken out between a few of the players, although not on the scale of the Battle of Longford! There was an almighty crash as the floor of our opposition's changing room gave way and the police were called. The club got a fine, but no one seemed to mind too much.

A couple of months before the next season started, Micky left Brighton for Leicester, a club which were playing in the Championship. It was a difficult decision for him as things were going so well at Brighton. We were lying fifth in League 1 and felt we had a good chance in the play-offs.

The players were genuinely sorry to see Micky go, but as always when this sort of thing happens, you just have to get on with it. Peter Taylor, who in more recent years has become better known as the manager who made David Beckham captain of England, took over. His main aim seemed to be not to rock the boat. He didn't need to get heavy in the changing room as the players did it for ourselves.

Brighton had some very strong personalities in the side at the time and that was part of the reason for the team's success. We also got on well with each other, which helped massively. No one got away with anything and everyone paid their fines if they put a step out of line, even me. By the end of the season we had quite a big kitty, which we blew on a night out.

New manager Peter and I fell out a couple of times, but that was only because he dropped me. I was fighting for my career, so I don't think he expected anything else. He helped the team win League 1 and then resigned at the end of the season. We couldn't believe his decision and I still don't understand it to this day.

Next up for the manager's job was Martin Hinshelwood. He had been a brilliant Head of Youth at the club for a number of years and a caretaker manager of the first team whenever he was asked. One of the problems for Hinsh—as we called him—was that the decision to make him manager was made at the end of the pre-season and he didn't have a chance to get his own team together.

On top of that our leading goal scorer, Bobby Zamora, was injured at the start of the season. After winning the first game and drawing the second, we lost game after game, and in the end the chairman had no choice but to bring in someone new. We all felt for Hinsh, though. The team's lack of success wasn't down to him.

After the thirteenth game of the season the club appointed Steve Coppell and he was one of the best managers I've ever played under because of his attention to detail. Steve's team talks on the day before a game were brilliant. He had his own video machine at home and he would put together footage showing how the opposition played. For example, he would show how a right winger always cut in on his left side, so our player at left back could be ready and waiting for the match the next day.

Sadly, Steve only lasted a season as manager. We were relegated, through no fault of his, and Reading came in with an offer for him that the club couldn't refuse. As any football fan knows, Steve's record with Reading after that speaks for itself.

Naturally we were all disappointed about getting relegated, especially as we'd nearly avoided it, but considering that we were playing in a temporary stadium we couldn't really expect to sustain a position in the Championship.

Dick Knight, our chairman, brought in Mark McGhee next, and despite having yet another change of manager, we still felt we had a realistic chance of going up again. Mark was all about hard work and being well-drilled. But he made an error, trying to make an impact and showing who was boss, by having a go at our captain, Danny Cullip. This was something he didn't need to do as Danny was a major reason for our success.

Having said that, in his first season Mark managed to get us to the play-off final against Bristol City at the Millennium Stadium in Cardiff. Apart from getting my first professional contract, this was the best day of my career. One of my strongest memories about the day was when my team-mate, Leon Knight, scored the goal that won us—Brighton—the final. Half of the 60,000 crowd stood in silence at one end of the ground while the other end erupted with joy. It was unbelievable.

The day before that amazing game, West Ham had played Crystal Palace in the Championship play-off final. A couple of Crystal Palace supporters then decided to spend all night ringing the hotel room I was staying in with Richard Carpenter (or Chippy as he is better known to his team-mates). For those of you who don't know, there's a great rivalry between Brighton and Palace fans. But, anyway . . . They managed to keep me and my team-mate up half the night and we were both really tired in the morning, which is obviously just what they wanted. Fortunately, Chippy and I still played well, so it didn't matter in the long run. Come on, you Seagulls!

But in football as in life, you have to take the hard knocks too. The worst moment in my career came a few seasons later, on Boxing Day 2006, ironically in a match against the team I've supported all my life, Queens Park Rangers. A few minutes into the game I got taken down by a very nasty tackle. My leg lay shattered beneath me. The pain was terrible and although I didn't realise it at the time, it meant the end of my career.

It would be the end of everything I had dreamed of doing in football. You can't imagine how hard that is to bear.

I don't have any hard feelings against Marcus Bean, the player who did the awful tackle, because although it was a foul, I don't think he intended it be anything more than that. I tried to get back to playing again, but by the pre-season of 2007 I had to call it a day. The worst day in a footballer's life is when you have to admit that it is over. It feels like the end of the world.

As well as the gut-wrenching feeling caused by the injury, other things made my football career end in a way I would never have wished. I don't feel that the Brighton manager at the time, Dean Wilkins, gave me as much respect as he could have done. When Dean was the youth team coach and I was in the first team we got on really well. Anyone who knows Dean will tell you that he's a fantastic coach and I would be the first to support that view. When he became manager of the first team, though, most of the top players, who had been so successful over the years for Brighton, were getting older and coming towards the end of their careers. Dean had to deal with that, which wasn't easy for us or him.

At first, whilst I was recovering from my injury, Dean let me come along to games and help in the changing room. Gradually, though, and without explanation, the invites to matches got fewer and fewer and I felt more and more isolated, which was difficult for me to deal with.

However Dean had behaved after my injury, it wouldn't have made any difference to whether or not I could have made a comeback, though. My career as a professional footballer was over.

CHAPTER EIGHT

READING MATTERS

It was when I was having treatment for another football injury back in 2003 that I got talking to our club physio Malcolm Stuart. I told him that as I was in my late twenties I was beginning to worry about what I would do once I was too old to be a professional footballer. A football career does not last long compared to most jobs. I knew I had to start thinking about the next stage in my life, but my big worry was that, after my lack of school, I still had problems with reading and writing. I was fretting that I'd struggle to get a job. Since leaving school I had swept these issues under the carpet, but that didn't mean they had gone away.

To a certain extent it was easy at home as my wife, Sonya, would sort out everything from shopping lists to paying the bills. As a football player I didn't have to do any writing, except for signing autographs, which I could manage—as long as people didn't want a special message or had a long or difficult name to spell. Even then I had found a way of getting round it. I just made sure one of the other players who knew about my issues with reading and writing was close by to help me.

So, for instance, I would say I had to nip off for a minute or two while my mate did the difficult bit, leaving me to add my signature. One way or another I used to manage.

I wasn't too bad at reading and I could just about manage with the *Sun* on the team bus on the way to matches. It wasn't as if the newspaper was the wrong way up and I was pretending to read it! Mind you, there were a few funny things that happened as a result.

Once I was on the motorway

following some mates to a reserve game at Brentford when, knowing the problems it would lead to, they turned off suddenly, leaving me on my own in the car. I ended up heading towards Luton because I couldn't read the signs to find my way back. I had to get on my mobile to find out which way to go and I got fined £50 by the football club for being late, which my mates thought was hilarious.

There were also plenty of not-so-funny times, such as feeling sad that I couldn't help my kids with their homework or reading; I always had to leave that to Sonya.

Malcolm Stuart, the club physio, understood my worries about my future and advised me to get in touch with Alan Sanders from Brighton and Hove Albion's community scheme. He was manager of the new study support centre at the club's Withdean ground. This centre ran courses for adults who struggled with maths and/or English and those people who wanted to learn the basics of how to use computers.

The idea behind having a study centre at a professional football club is simple. People who didn't do well at school and think learning is for other people are less likely to be scared off by going along to somewhere like a football club than going along to a college or something like that.

I have to say that the 'feel' of the centre at Brighton is very relaxed and unthreatening. The people who go along there don't have to like football. They go because they want to and are made to feel comfortable there. I know loads of people who have been to the centre and gone on to bigger and better things as a result. It's not all about reading, writing and adding up, really. It's all about confidence and a belief in yourself.

As I was a current football player

at Brighton, I didn't want the world to know that I struggled with reading and writing. So the centre gave me lessons on my own, away from everyone else. For anyone reading this who has faced the same difficulties, I'll just say it should be easier for you than me to take that great step. Because, probably, you are not in the public eye, I hope you won't need, so much, to hide away.

I found that when I was given tasks about reading and writing, I wasn't as bad at them as I thought I'd be. I gradually started to gain more confidence with my reading, and when I began to guess at what the more difficult words sounded like, more often than not I was right. I was able to write, too, but it was painfully slow. But once I started, that too has improved with practice. I didn't have to bother too much with numeracy as I was always quite good with numbers, especially when it came to people owing me money!

Whichever football club I played for, you see, I was always in charge of the club fines. Every team has a set of rules given to players by the manager and coaches at the beginning of each season. For example, you must always remember to bring the right training gear with you and you must never be late. The fines were quite steep and players could end up owing a few hundred quid at the end of the month if they disobeyed the rules. If team members refused to pay the fines, the money owed was taken out of their wages. The money taken in this way always went towards paying for a players' holiday at the end of the season.

You can imagine what lengths players would go to in order to avoid paying these fines. They were always trying to baffle me with figures, but I was having none of it. The more money I could get out of them, the better the holiday to come. As you can imagine, I always managed to be one of the players who paid the least!

*   *   *

Anyway, back to me and my reading. I got into the habit of going for lessons once a week, but thinking back I think I should have made more of an effort. To start with my progress was pretty slow, although I was pleased that I'd plucked up the courage to go along to learn at the centre at all.

The more I got to know my tutor, Alan, the more comfortable I became with the whole situation. After a few weeks, he asked if I would 'go public' and admit to my struggles with reading and writing. This was a massive step for me and not one I was prepared to do without a lot of soul-searching. I was a professional footballer! It was a horrible feeling for me to come out and tell thousands of people about the things I found hard to do.

In the end, though, I felt that by 'going public' I'd be paying the club back for helping me, and hopefully other people would follow my example. After finally agreeing to 'confess', the national press came to Brighton's Withdean Stadium to cover the story. *The Times* wrote a two-page article and I was also on regional television and radio. For me to sit there and speak to the media about my problems with reading and writing shows just how much confidence I'd gained already. It was hardly the image of the ex-prisoner and football 'hard man' Charlie Oatway the media knew!

Just about every professional footballer's contract says they are expected to do up to eight hours of community work a week for their club. In my experience only a few ever do, and that's probably limited to one or two hours a week at the most. I was doing a lot more than that because I enjoyed it. The club's community scheme got some funding (£1.7 million to be precise!) to expand their work across the whole county of Sussex and I became an official learning champion.

This honour meant that I opened a few of the new study centres as well as meeting and talking to adult learners as and when I could. We managed to get people interested in learning all sorts and thousands of adults got themselves some proper qualifications too. It gave me a real sense of worth knowing that I could help other people, so they wouldn't have to struggle to overcome their fears as much as I had done.

Not only that, but the chairman of Brighton at the time, Dick Knight, told me there would be a job for me at the club after I'd finished playing, which was great to hear. I had always got on well with Dick, who really looked after his players, apart from on one occasion when we'd just been promoted to the Championship. My agent was trying to get the best deal he could for me, so he pointed out to Dick that not only had I helped the club get promoted, but I was also the captain of the team.

My agent explained to the chairman that being captain gave me a lot of extra responsibility, which meant I should be paid more. Dick's reply was, 'Well, how about we don't make him captain then, and we can pay him what I suggested.' Thanks, Dick!

*   *   *

In 2005, my tutor Alan was approached by someone from the Football Association (FA) who was starting up a programme called 'Heading for Success'. The purpose of this was to try to get adults who struggled with maths and English to come to football clubs to learn, in the same way as we'd been doing at

Brighton. Before I knew it we were both being whizzed up to FA headquarters in Soho Square to promote the new scheme. I knew where the FA headquarters were, as I'd been there a few times for hearings when I'd been sent off the pitch in matches, but it was nice to be going there when they weren't having a go at me!

I'd been told by Alan that I would have to answer a few questions from former footballer Garth Crooks in front of the media and other guests. When it came to it, however, Garth just introduced me and sat down. Everyone clapped as I hobbled up onto the stage (I was on crutches after breaking my leg in that game against QPR). It was then that I realised he had no intention of asking me any questions, but was waiting for me to make a speech. I looked towards my tutor Alan, who was in the front row with his head in his hands. I could have bloody killed him. I'm still not sure to this day whether or not he set me up, though he assures me he didn't.

Anyway, there was no going back, so I spoke for about ten minutes, balancing on my crutches, telling everyone about my problems with reading and writing. I got a standing ovation at the end, but I'm not sure if it was because of my ability as a speech-maker or because they felt sorry for me.

Soon after this, Brighton's chairman, Dick Knight, told me he was at some PFA (the Professional Footballers' Association) event and a chairman of an Italian football club was sitting next to him. When Dick introduced himself, the Italian said, 'Oh, you must be the chairman of the club where the player has just said he can't read and write.' Word certainly gets around quickly!

Playing football is what I always wanted to do and it is much more enjoyable than talking to the public about my problems with dyslexia! But I'm glad that I've been able to make a difference to some people's lives as a result. I don't claim to have sorted everything out as far as my reading is concerned, but I am getting there. At least I'm now able to help my kids a little bit, which is a start. And now even Charlie Oatway has written a book! Whoever would have believed that I'd do that?

CHAPTER NINE

LIFE GOES ON!

The end of my career as a professional footballer was a real blow for me. I was desperate to carry on playing. I spent many months trying to get back into the game after I broke my leg. Although it was beginning to dawn on me that I might not make it, I couldn't afford to be negative.

My accident happened at the start of the 2007/08 season. I had played in a couple of pre-season 'friendly' games, but in order to play I had to have an injection of cortisone beforehand, to ease my pain. This made me speak to the club doc, Tim Stevenson, and he said that if I carried on playing I might have real problems walking as I got older.

In the early part of August, as at

every club, the team were called to the ground one afternoon for the new season photo. This completely screwed me up as I couldn't decide what to do. If I went in for the photo, I would feel as though I was cheating the fans, as I didn't really know if I would play again. On the other hand, not going in for the photo was pretty much me saying that was it.

Time was running out as the team was beginning to assemble, so I phoned my literacy tutor, Alan Sanders, who by this time had become a bit of a mentor to me. He felt I should listen to doctor Tim, call it a day and come and work for Albion in the Community (Brighton football club's community scheme). I also spoke to Dean Wilkins, the manager, and he said it was my decision, so I said, 'OK, that's it, I'll have to pack it in.'

I hobbled round the corner away from everyone else and just cried. I know it doesn't go with my image, but no matter how well I thought I had prepared for that moment, I just couldn't take it. It was the end of the dream as far as I was concerned, and I cannot describe the panic, despair and worry I felt after realising that my career in football was over. I was in a desperate state. I just cried and cried some more.

I don't know what I would have done if Alan, my brilliant tutor, hadn't given me the support I needed. He told me that the best thing to do was not dwell on the end and try to get straight into my new job with the community scheme. He said I should spend the next few weeks getting to understand what the role was all about. It was great that they broke me in gently, but it was still a culture shock. I mean, they wouldn't even let me have a kip in the afternoon, which I always used to do when I was a player!

As I came to terms with this massive life change, I knew I had to make some quick decisions. For a start, I still wanted to be involved with playing football in some way, even though I knew it wouldn't be at Brighton. Also, as grateful as I was for my new job with Albion in the Community, it meant taking a 50 per cent pay cut from my playing contract.

I knew that I could still just about play football, so long as I didn't have to train. At a professional club, you can't get away with that, but I could at semi-pro level. I started to look around a couple of clubs and it was then that Tony Clark, who worked for Albion in the Community, got Ian Baird, the manager of Havant & Waterlooville, to give me a ring. I signed with them as a player and everything went really well for a few weeks, but even better was to follow!

Ian Baird decided to jump ship and go to manage a football club along the coast at Eastleigh as they had more money to spend. The assistant manager at Havant—Shaun Gale—was given the job in Ian's place. He asked me to be his first-team coach and extended my contract from one year to two. I couldn't believe my luck and began to think there might be a life outside of professional football after all.

Although we were only just above mid-table in our league, the Conference South, we started to do well in the FA Cup, winning a couple of first and second round matches before being drawn away to York, who were a division higher. We managed to scrape an unexpected win against them and were then drawn away against a league club, Notts County. Incredibly, we beat them too and drew Swansea away in the third round.

Before that match, I went to see Swansea play and, to be honest, I thought they could be beaten. This third-round game had a bit of extra spice for me as I had played for

Cardiff in earlier days and I knew some of the Swansea supporters would know this. Sure enough, I got a lot of abuse, but I didn't care because we got away with a 1–1 draw. To take them back to Havant for a replay was unbelievable.

The only problem for the club was that fixtures were piling up fast as we weren't able to play our league games because of the cup matches. A couple of days before we were due to play the cup replay against Swansea there was a league game scheduled. This was really bad news as a few of our players were injured.

Unbelievably, Havant's league game had to be called off because our pitch was flooded after a freak rainstorm, an incident the referee described as 'a minor miracle'. Rumours that the club had hired a couple of fire engines to flood the pitch are totally untrue!

A second 'miracle' then followed when we beat Swansea 4–2 in the replay. There was a fair bit of national media attention for the game as Swansea were in League 1, and chasing promotion, which they eventually got. But the attention was nothing compared to what we were about to receive when we were drawn away to Liverpool Football Club in the fourth round of the Cup.

As the first-team coach and one of the only ex-professional players at Havant, I received much of the media spotlight. I did a daily column in the *Sun* for a few days based on our build-up and was also interviewed by Helen Chamberlain on *Soccer AM* for Sky Television on the morning of the match.

The game really caught the country's imagination as it could have been one of those great FA Cup upsets, especially as we were 1–0 up at one point and drawing 2–2 at half-time. I was on the bench as I was carrying an injury and I was also keen for some of the younger players to experience playing at Anfield.

At the start of the second half, Liverpool started to get edgy, and rightly so. I was sitting close to their star-players, Steven Gerrard and Jamie Carragher, and I heard Gerrard lean across to his mate and say, 'Come on, we'd better warm up.' I thought at the time, well, Havant can bring on me and Liverpool can bring on Gerrard and Carragher! Not much difference there then.

As it happened all three of us came on to play and we, Havant, ended up losing 4–2, although the result had nothing to do with the substitutions! After the game, my mate Bobby Zamora arranged for Liverpool's Yossi Benayoun to give me his shirt, which had been signed by all of the players. I managed to raise quite a few quid for Albion in the Community with that.

The whole day, and in fact the next few days, was like a dream. It was so unbelievable. Havant were on the back pages of all of the Sunday newspapers and were special guests at the next day's Man United game at Old Trafford. I was even interviewed live on ITV at half-time with Havant captain, Jamie Collins.

*   *   *

I lasted one more season at Havant and overall they were two fantastic years that I will always remember. I have to thank Shaun Gale for making me his first-team coach. I left under a bit of a cloud because of a dispute over my contract, but that didn't take anything away from the fantastic people I met during that time.

It gave me my first taste of coaching a team and it was a great experience. There's no doubt that semi-professionals are animals of a different sort to full-time players. Football isn't the be-all and end-all for them, for obvious reasons. I found that difficult to cope with at times as I tried to get the players to give it their all. While many of them tried, there were far too many who just seemed to be in it for the extra wages, and that really frustrated me.

My main area of concern and disbelief at this level of football was the type of opposition manager you got. Some of them were OK, but others were really full of themselves, far more than the players they were managing. It was as if they thought they were world famous when in fact no one outside of their home town had heard of them.

Some of these managers' tactics left a lot to be desired, too. There was one who used to openly encourage his players to injure the opposition. I couldn't believe the match officials didn't say anything as he shouted such instructions from the sidelines. I never saw anything like it in the professional game. Unbelievable!

Before I got involved with Havant, I decided to get my coaching qualifications. The summer before I joined the team I got my Level 1 badge, which was pretty straight-forward, but when I looked into doing Level 2, I realised there would be a fair amount of writing to do. I knew the FA would have supported me because they knew I struggled with reading and writing, but in the end I persuaded my literacy tutor, Alan Sanders, to do the badge with me.

As an ex-PE teacher, Alan was happy to join me as his coaching badges were out of date. I'm really glad we did it together as we had a great laugh and he made sure it wasn't a big drama for me, with my difficulties, in front of other people.

At the time I started the course I had just come off crutches after breaking my leg, which meant I couldn't do some of the football demonstrations. Alan loved that because I got marked down when I was supposed to demonstrate the lofted pass. He made out that I couldn't do it even before I got injured, which the other lads found very funny. Thanks, Al!

In the end we both passed that qualification and decided to do the Level 3 (or UEFA 'B') badge the following spring. There were twenty-four of us on that course, and as one of only two ex-professionals (the other being John Piercy, ex-Spurs and Brighton), everyone chose me for the demos. When it came to the final practical assessment, though, once again I couldn't do it.

I'd had to go into hospital the night before as my knee was in agony. Alan claimed I'd bottled it, of course, and went on to pass the exam with flying colours.

I got to take my exam a couple of

months later and passed first time around. Of that group of twenty-four, I think only five passed first time, so it's definitely not easy. I had found keeping a file of my work a bit difficult, but I struggled through and was given extra time for the theory exam because of my dyslexia. In the end, I got a higher score than Alan for that bit. To think he once used to teach kids!

I still keep up with a few of the lads I met then. We had people of all shapes and sizes. It doesn't matter what you look like and you don't have to be fit to give it a go and succeed.

There was one guy, for instance, we nicknamed Dawn French as he looked and ran just like her. He gave out as much stick as he received, though, so don't go feeling sorry for him!

CHAPTER TEN

HEADING FOR SUCCESS

Working for Albion in the Community was a real learning curve. When I started I'd often think, 'Hang on a minute, Charlie Oatway working in an office? Are you sure?' I have to admit it wasn't a natural way forward for me, but I seemed to be able to adapt. There were loads of things to get involved with. At the time the scheme was growing rapidly, with twenty-six full-time staff and over a hundred part-timers. The two directors, Alan Sanders and Steve Ford, decided to make six people heads of departments, and I was one of them.

Alan has always said that it's a shame to lose professionals from the game of football just because they've stopped playing. He realised that players often have more to offer, not only in obvious areas like football coaching, but because they are usually highly driven individuals who are capable of doing other things. Personally, I think Alan's view is spot on.

I really appreciate Alan and Steve for having faith in me and giving me the job at Albion in the Community. I got on particularly well with Alan and we have since become really good mates. This is even more surprising when you consider my somewhat dodgy background and his academic upbringing. In itself, this shows what a long way I've come, to become close friends with people from all walks of life and not just my own. Perhaps that's one of the secrets of my success.

My department for Albion in the Community was called Community Relations, and my job involved going to senior management meetings with the other managers and two directors every three or four weeks. I was quite nervous at the first meeting because everyone is expected to give a departmental update. I noticed one or two of the others give me a smile as my turn approached, but I coped OK. I think they liked me coming to the meetings because I gave everyone a bit of stick (except my real bosses, the directors, of course!).

In fact, within a few weeks of getting the job I had given nicknames to quite a few of the staff, which some liked more than others. We had such a laugh in the office that when people phoned up I'm sure they thought there was a party going on. I remember one time I was having a friendly fight with Ric, who was one of the coaching staff, and we were rolling around on the office floor. Alan walked in and I thought I'd get a right telling off. He came towards us and instead of going ballistic, as I expected, he just stepped over us without saying a word and started to make some phone calls. Ric and I soon got up and got on with our work out of sheer embarrassment. I whacked him a couple more times, of course, but he didn't dare make a noise.

Having said that, it wasn't all about having a laugh and I was struck by how hard everyone within the scheme works. That suited me because I'm not someone who likes to hang around not doing much. In many ways the sort of humour we shared was similar to what you find in the training ground, only more watered down. You have to be careful not to swear too much as other people in the office might be on the phone and the last thing they want is some slanging match going on in the background.

One of the things I really liked about the job was the variety of projects I was able to get involved with. As well as the community work,

I coached two of the local sixth-form football teams. One of the senior teachers at City College Brighton and Hove, Dave Williams, came up with the idea of me being a mentor to some of the students who weren't doing so well for one reason or another. This turned out to be so successful that when other ex-players came on board, Guy Butters, Danny Cullip and Richard (Chippy) Carpenter, we were able to sort out similar deals for them with other colleges.

We were also mentors for a project based on getting people with low qualifications back into work, which included a course called Personal Best. The idea was that everyone who completed the course would be guaranteed an interview for a job working on London 2012. We basically helped people complete the course, then helped them into employment, further education or voluntary work.

115

After that I got involved in another European project working with similar organisations in France. We teamed up with Le Havre football club because the ex-Brighton player and all-time hero of mine when he used to play for QPR, John Byrne, used to play for them. We shared community projects and it worked really well for both clubs. I went over there quite a few times and we still have a great relationship. We've even had a few of their players come over and play for us.

We also worked hard on raising money through events like a night at the dogs and a fun run. As I said before, I'm good at getting people to give me what they owe. I bullied all of the current Brighton professionals to turn up and pay their way.

*   *   *

Of course, I am still a 'right little Charlie' and problems still come my way now and then. I had a bit of a falling out with Darren Teague, one of the other department managers, which ended up with me having a real go at him. It was the only way I knew to deal with disputes and I deeply regret it. I regard Darren as a really good friend now and I've learned to deal with things differently from the changing-room justice I was used to.

This incident happened shortly before a couple of others I could have done without. The first one happened when I was with Sonya, who had been helping out at Albion in the Community, when we were having a drink after work. We went to this pub and a few blokes I vaguely knew started giving me stick and being rude to Sonya. That was something I wasn't prepared to take, so I said to one of them that we should discuss it outside. As soon as I walked out I was jumped on by four of them and ended up in hospital.

Why do people feel the need to do this and why do four blokes need to take on one person? People have asked me if I intend to do anything about the incident, but to be honest I'd rather forget about it.

The other unfortunate event to happen that summer was when I stayed at Alan's house with my family while he went on holiday. To cut a long story short, Sonya and I locked ourselves out and couldn't get back in. It was a bit embarrassing as Alan had warned me to be careful about this and I had told him not to worry; that coming from my background there wasn't a house built that I couldn't get into if I wanted!

I went around the back of the house to look for an open window while Sonya stayed at the front. The next thing I heard was Sonya screaming in pain. She had tried to climb up to a first-floor window and had crashed down on to the driveway. She ended up in hospital for three months with a broken hip and a broken wrist and we were worried she might not be able to walk properly again. What a summer! As it happened she is now OK, but Alan has charged me for cracking the tarmac on the driveway.

*   *   *

By now you might think I'm not the right person to look after a football team, but in the 2009/10 season I began helping with the Brighton first team under the manager Russell Slade. When Gus Poyet took over from Russell halfway through the season, I was made first-team coach. My mates think they only made me coach so I could intimidate the players into doing what they're told (a bit like Sir Alex Ferguson!), but I think there's more to it than that because I know what the players can and can't get away with. Having a few hundred games under my belt helps me gain respect. We're moving in the right direction.

So that's my story. I came from rock bottom as a kid with no hope and became a man who is happily married with a fantastic job in football. I don't pretend for a minute that I won't have any scrapes in the future, but I do know I'm in a better position than ever to know how to deal with anything that comes along. I can safely say that it won't end with me being banged up in jail. There you are, Dad, I did listen to you after all!